Hummingbirds

by Betty John

ILLUSTRATIONS BY BILL BARSS

FOLLETT PUBLISHING COMPANY

CHICAGO

Rubythroat Hummingbird

Hummingbirds are the smallest birds in the world.

They get their name from the humming sound their wings make when they fly.

Their wings beat so fast you can not see them move.

Hummingbirds are found only in North and South America.

There are about 500 different kinds.

Most hummingbirds live in those parts of South America that are very hot.

Underwood's Hummingbird

Sappho Hummingbird

Mexican Shear-tail

Fewer and fewer hummingbirds are found as one goes north.

There are 149 different kinds in Mexico, Texas, and California.

Only one kind, the Rubythroat, lives east of the Rocky Mountains in the United States and Canada.

7

Helena's, or Fairy Hummingbird

One of the smallest hummingbirds, the
Fairy Hummingbird of Cuba, is a little
more than two inches long, from the end of
its bill to the tip of its tail.

The biggest, the Swordbearer of the
Andes, has a body three inches long and a
five-inch bill.

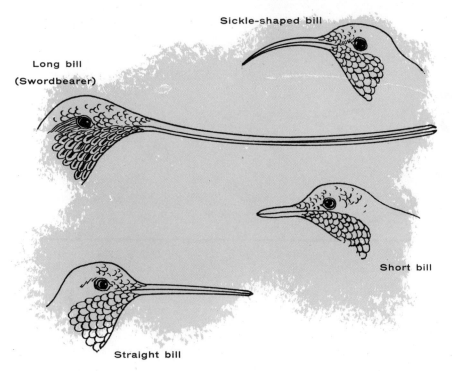

Sickle-shaped bill

Long bill
(Swordbearer)

Short bill

Straight bill

Some hummingbirds have long bills.
Some have short bills.

Some have curved bills. Most
hummingbirds have long, straight bills.
All the bills are very thin.

The different bills help hummingbirds
to get food from different kinds of flowers.
Can you see why the Swordbearer feeds in
long flowers?

9

Anna's Hummingbird

Eared Hummingbird

Swallow-tailed Hummingbird

Of all the birds in the world, hummingbirds are the brightest in color.

Some are a rich dark green. Some are bright green with red and white. Some are purple.

Some can change their color from red-brown to purple to red. Some have blue throats, black chins, or red bibs.

Their colors flash when they fly about in the sunlight.

Mother Rubythroat with nest and eggs.

The mother hummingbird lays only two
little white eggs. They look like beans.

Before she lays her eggs, she makes a
nest that looks like a tiny cup. The inside
of the nest is very soft. It is made from
milkweed silk and bits of down from other
plants.

The outside of the nest is covered
with moss and other plants, held together
by spider webs.

This makes the nest look like a knob
on a tree. The nest is held to the tree
by spider webs.

The mother bird makes her nest
without the help of the father bird.

Mother Black-chinned Hummingbird

Baby Hummingbirds in nest.

It takes about two weeks for baby birds to come from the eggs.

The baby birds are very little when they are born.

They are blind and helpless and very ugly.

They have almost no feathers at all.

Mother Rubythroat Hummingbird and babies in nest.

The mother hummingbird feeds her babies
by putting her bill, with the food in it,
way down the baby's throat.

She feeds them small spiders, small
insects, and the nectar from flowers.

She hovers, or stays in one place in
the air, while she feeds her babies. She can
do this without falling because she moves
her wings so fast.

In about three weeks the babies are as big as grown-up birds.

Now they have a full coat of gray and white feathers.

It will take about nine months for them to grow a full coat of bright colored feathers.

Soon they are flying as fast as the father and mother birds.

Mother Rubythroat and young birds.

Trumpet vine   Bergamot   Coral honeysuckle   Phlox

Hummingbirds need insects and nectar to give them strength for flying.

Most flowers make and store nectar deep down inside the flower.

Nectar is like perfumed sweet water.

Each flower has its own perfume and color.

Hummingbirds like the color red.

16

Father Calliope Hummingbird

Columbine

Larkspur

Wild honeysuckle

The sun helps the flowers to make their nectar.

The sun puts a lot of energy into each little drop.

When hummingbirds eat insects and sip nectar, this food gives their little bodies energy.

It gives them the strength to fly.

Hummingbirds are very strong for their size.

Hummingbirds must have food about every twenty minutes.

They work so hard making their wings go fast that they use up their food very quickly.

That is why they have to eat so often.

They are tireless little fliers.

As long as they can find enough food, they can keep on flying fast all day.

They can fly straight up, down or sideways, and change to any direction in mid-air.

How hummingbirds' wings move.

The Father Rubythroat feeding.

Hummingbirds are the only birds that can hover, or stay in one place in the air, and back up in mid-air.

When hummingbirds sip nectar, they hover right in front of the flowers.

They never touch the flowers with their feet or wings.

They put their long bills down into the flowers. Their tongues are like little tubes.

They use their tongues to suck up nectar.

Hummingbird's bill and tongue much enlarged to show barbs.

Most hummingbirds have tiny barbs, or brushes, at the end of their long tongues.

These barbs help the hummingbird to sweep up any insect that is inside the flower.

In this way the hummingbird gets nectar and insects from the flower at the same time.

Hummingbirds, like bees, help make more flowers.

A flower must have pollen from another flower to make new flowers. Pollen is a very fine yellow powder that is found in each flower.

Hummingbirds help carry pollen from one flower to another. Their wings make a breeze which blows pollen from flower to flower.

White-eared Hummingbird

Mother Rubythroat with nest and eggs.

Of all the hummingbirds, the Rubythroat
is the one most people know best.

That is because more people can see
Rubythroats.

In summer Rubythroats live in the
eastern half of the United States.

In the winter they live in Central
America.

Father Rubythroat and young birds.

The father Rubythroat is between three
and four inches long from the end of
his bill to the tip of his tail.

He is bright green, with a white breast.

Under his black bill, he wears a
bright red bib.

This is his ruby throat that flashes
and glows.

The mother Rubythroat has no ruby
throat. Her throat is all white.

Rubythroats among garden flowers.

You will hear the hum of a Rubythroat before you see him flying about among your flowers.

When he hovers in front of a flower to sip nectar, you can not see his wings at all.

He looks like a lovely jewel hanging from the sky on an invisible thread.

Rubythroats and different kinds of feeders.

To bring Rubythroats to your garden, you must have food for them. To feed them, buy little glass tubes at the drug store or bird feeders at the pet store.

Fill the glass feeders with sugar water, colored with a little red food coloring.

Then tie the feeders to branches of trees or bushes in the yard.

If the feeders are kept filled with sugar water all summer, many hummingbirds may come to visit them.

25

Sometimes Rubythroats sound as if they were scolding each other.

But they are not. They never fight among themselves.

They have no real enemies.

They are not afraid of people.

But the mother hummingbird will fight anything, if she thinks it will harm her babies.

She uses her long sharp bill like a dagger.

For her size, she is the bravest bird in the world.

The Mother Rubythroat protects her nest.

A Rubythroat family flying together.

Most of the time Rubythroats fly at about 50 miles an hour.

They have been known to fly as fast as 75 miles an hour.

It takes a lot of strength to go that fast.

Mother Rubythroat and young birds in Central America.

There are only three or four other kinds of birds that fly as far as the Rubythroats each spring and each fall.

Just before the flowers dry up in September, the Rubythroats set out for Central America, many, many miles away.

Even baby Rubythroats only five months old must fly far away to the flowers of Central America.

In March or early April they begin
to fly back to the United States and
Canada.

They fly right back to the tree where
they were born.

They fly back each spring to build
their nests, lay their eggs, and raise
more bright little Rubythroats.

Rubythroat Hummingbirds in North America.

Words Younger Children May Need Help With
(Numbers refer to page on which the word first appears.)

5	hummingbirds	**9**	curved	**18**	tireless
6	north		straight		sideways
	South America	**11**	milkweed		direction
7	Mexico	**12**	moss	**19**	tongues
	Texas		spider	**20**	barbs
	California		web		brushes
	Rubythroat	**14**	insects	**21**	pollen
	Rocky Mountains		nectar	**22**	eastern
	United States		hovers	**24**	jewel
	Canada				invisible
8	Cuba	**16**	strength	**25**	branches
	Swordbearer		perfumed	**28**	Central America
	Andes	**17**	energy		

THINGS TO DO IN THE CLASSROOM OR AT HOME

Visit a zoological park that has birds in it. Look for the hummingbirds. See their small size and their long bills. Make a list of all the colors each bird has.

If there is a Rubythroat hummingbird, look for the beautiful bright green coat, the black bill, the white breast with the bright red ruby under its bill. If there is a mother Rubythroat, look for the all-white breast.

When the hummingbird flies, listen to the wings hum as the wings move quickly. See how the hummingbird can fly in every direction. If the hummingbird flies very quickly, you will hardly be able to see its wings moving.

Is there a hummingbird nest? See how soft it is inside, and how much the nest looks like part of the tree branch.

Watch how the hummingbird gets its food, staying in one place in the air.

Go to a wooded area and look for birds. Sit quietly for a while until the birds become used to you. Watch how they get their food and eat it. See where they fly with their food. This will tell you where they live.

Make a list of the different birds you see and describe their size, color, bills, and feeding habits. Try to find their nests. Do not come too close to the nests. The birds will fly at you if there are eggs or baby birds in the nest.

Some birds build nests in trees, others near bushes, and others in open fields. How are their nests built? Are the nests well-made or just put together? What did the birds use to build their nests? Is it hard to see the nests far away? Every nest seems to look just like the things near it.

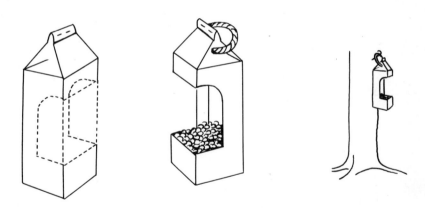

Make a feeding center for birds. This can be done in the spring for all birds or in the winter for birds that do not go away in the winter. Put food in a few places for the birds to eat. Birds like bread crumbs, chicken feed, all kinds of seeds, and suet. Suet is hard fat, and you can get it at the meat store.

You can make a bird feeder with an empty milk carton. Wash the carton and dry it. Cut away the front part as shown.

Then make two holes near the top, put a strong string through them, and knot the string.

In the spring put out things that the birds can use for nests. Straws, twigs, cotton, string, and small feathers are just fine. Birdhouses and birdbaths will help too.

Have the children read and learn about the different kinds of bills, feet, tails, and wings that birds have. See how each kind is helpful to birds according to the way they live and what they eat.

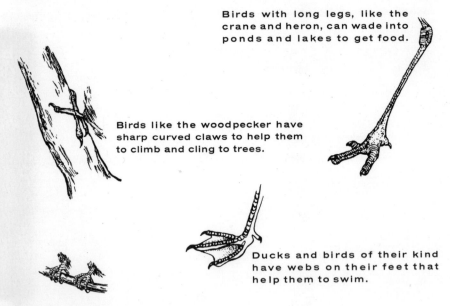

Birds with long legs, like the crane and heron, can wade into ponds and lakes to get food.

Birds like the woodpecker have sharp curved claws to help them to climb and cling to trees.

Ducks and birds of their kind have webs on their feet that help them to swim.

The hummingbird's tiny feet are used only for clinging to little twigs and stems.

Have the children learn the different ways that birds protect themselves from their enemies.

Make a list of the ways birds help and harm us.